The Balance Finder

SHERRICE THOMAS

REFRESHING STREAMS, INC.
GAHANNA, OHIO

THE BALANCE FINDER

For more information, contact:

Refreshing Streams, Inc.
947 Johnstown Road #129
Gahanna, Ohio 43230
(614) 496-1143

www.refreshingstreams.org

Layout by: A Reader's Perspective

Library of Congress Control Number 201090884
ISBN 978-0-9826727-0-9

Acknowledgements

First, I give honor to God, the creator of the universe, for releasing the divine revelation of balance into my life.

My husband, Frederick J. Thomas, Jr. Your love and ongoing support is more valuable to me than you'll ever know.

My parents, Aaron and Charlene Sledge, for spending countless nights ensuring I didn't smash my glasses or sleep on my books, in the early days of my writing life.

My son, Brian Sledge, for putting up with me writing at your practices and all through the night.

My sister, Kalimba Carter, for being such a cool sister who will share my work with anyone who will listen.

My friends and fellow authors, Dasaya Cates and Janice Redman, who both edited the first draft.

N. Kali Mincy, owner of Coaching Great Writers, for helping me "shape" the original draft via a great critique.

Tia Ross, the Black Writers Reunion and Conference (BWRC) producer/director for providing an avenue for authors to connect and learn.

The community of authors on Facebook and Twitter, who encouraged me and shared a plethora of resources.

The Balance Finder

Table of Contents

Superwoman is for Girls 1

   A Tale of Imbalance 3

The Origin of Imbalance 7

   Prelude 9

   Radical Feminism 11

   Independent Woman Syndrome 15

   The American Dream 19

   Balance Check 21

   Moment of Reflection 23

A State of Balance... 25

   Prelude 27

   Power to Decide 29

   Emotional Equilibrium 31

   Harmonious Arrangement 37

   Balance Check 39

   Moment of Reflection 41

Balance Enhancements 43

   Prelude 45

Spiritual Alignment 47

Mental Colonic 53

Guilt Detox 50 57

Balance Check 61

Moment of Reflection 63

B

Superwoman is for Girls

• • •

A Tale of Imbalance

WHY ME? My life is falling apart," Cindy screamed.
Despite her cries of frustration, her children refused to listen. In fact, Joah, her five-year old son, sat with his eyes glued to the TV, knowing he should be eating his breakfast.

Wait a minute. He's not even allowed to watch TV in the morning.

To make matters worse, Cindy's nine-year old daughter, Bri leaped around the living room like a ballerina instead of getting dressed.

"Look here, young lady! You better stop before you fall. And remind me why you're not dressed again?"

Devon, the oldest, firmly grasps a sleek game controller as he kills beings from another planet.

"Where did you get that game? You know we don't allow killing games in this house. Give it here and go brush your teeth! Now!"

Cindy glances at the clock and shakes her head as tears

flow from her eyelids.

How am I going to get them ready and drop them off at school in enough time to make it to work?

She flips through her planner only to find she's booked all day and will have to eat lunch walking from one meeting to the next or not at all. Not to mention, both Joah and Bri have soccer games this evening and their uniforms are still dirty. Devon has a chess club meeting and will have no ride home because Cindy has to be at two soccer games.

Who schedules two soccer games on a Thursday? Obviously, someone with nothing better to do!

"Mom!" Devon screams from the upstairs bathroom. "I forgot to tell you. Dad's working late, tonight."

"Oh shoot! I can't believe I forgot."

As she rushed to get her day in order, Cindy sniffed to hold back the tears. "I guess I'll do it all like I always do. I am Superwoman."

● ● ●

Cindy's story sounds familiar to many of us. Just think about how many times it seemed like there wasn't enough time in one day to accomplish everything on your plate. Leaping tall buildings in one single bound is seemingly impossible with only twenty-four hours to spare, especially, if you're supposed to sleep for at least eight. What's a woman to do? Look at the sky! It's a bird! It's a plane! It's Superwoman! No silly, Superwoman is for little girls! You, my friend, are a balanced woman. So, what's the difference?

- A superwoman operates in her own strength, while a balanced woman operates in divine strength.

- A superwoman lives a double life, while a balanced woman lives one.

- A superwoman seeks to save the world, while a balanced woman knows her role.

- A superwoman has all the answers all of the time, while a balanced woman understands she's on a lifelong journey of learning.

Being a balanced woman is about working towards gaining a spiritual alignment with the cosmos according to God's plan for your life. When you flow with the right stream of energy, your struggles aren't the same. I encourage you to enjoy this journey as you become a refreshed woman full of wisdom and balance. Embrace the divine strategies and I promise you'll achieve supernatural results.

The Origin of Imbalance

• • •

Prelude

THE PLAN to eradicate the Superwoman mentality goes against the grain most of our viewpoints. Our society encourages overachieving behavior and we embrace it just to fit in. Several celebrities have made beautiful songs that are odes to the Superwoman and have become almost as popular as the national anthem. Changing our mindset on this topic will definitely require major mental surgery.

In order to move past this mentality and adopt one that's new, we must understand how the situation came to be. That's why it's important for us to explore the origin of imbalance. On this leg of our journey, we'll focus on three key elements; Radical Feminism, Independent Woman Syndrome, and American Dream. Each element started with a good intention then for whatever reason, ended up having a negative impact on our society.

Radical Feminism

ORMER FIRST lady Eleanor Roosevelt once said, "No one can make you inferior without your consent." While her declaration rings true, we can't deny the reality of female inferiority as prescribed by the patriarchal system. The same applies to people of any color other than white.

Our ancestors can vouch for this societal nightmare because they experienced it in this country's infancy. Let's take a trip back in time to meet Mama Ruby, who worked on a cotton field of a southern plantation for forty-five years in blazing hot heat. Bending over in the to pull those white, fluffy balls off the green plant left her with a contorted spine. The pain forces her to walk hunched over with a limp. Her once smooth, coffee colored hands reflect the scar-filled gifts of poking cotton burrs. If you sat down with Mama Ruby to have a tall glass of cold lemonade, you'd learn that she never received a paycheck for all the years of her hard work. To make matters worse, her birth name isn't Ruby. That's what the master called her on the auction block.

She's not even from this country and her master expected her to be patriotic on Independence Day. Many moons ago, she was playing in a flower-laden field with her sister circle, when a few warriors from a neighboring tribe put a bag over her head and gave her to some white man. They stripped her of her regal beads and beat her senseless. Then, they forced her to ride on a gigantic boat for what seemed like forever. She'd tell you the story of how her master sold her children to an indigo farmer in the Caribbean even though he was their father. She'd been his secret and unwilling lover since the tender age of thirteen. Mama Ruby gave birth to their first child at only fourteen years of age. She didn't have the opportunity to live a balanced life because someone else was in control. Forced to be a Superwoman, Mama Ruby died crying out to God in her spirit because the fight had been beaten out of her.

When I mourn for Mama Ruby's pain, she reminds me that she's not alone. She shares the stories of many others. She's seen systematic barring of women from the voting process and homemakers who went to work when their husbands went off to fight the world war. These women worked the same jobs as their spouses and their pockets were much thinner. A woman wasn't worth the same money as a man to the factory owner.

For years, we've held our heads up high despite the injustice. As a result, some of us didn't mutter a mumbling word, others cowered under the pressure, and those remaining stood up for our rights. These scenarios reflect just a few of the atrocities that led to the various feminist movements. In the beginning, the focus was suffrage. The next phase of the movement was about breaking the inequality of the pay gap between men and women. The third phase took on the cause of reproductive rights. Keep in mind, these three areas of concern definitely overlapped.

Our feminist ancestors fought for what they felt was rightfully theirs and now women have the right to vote, the pay gaps between men and women closed a little, and we have a joint role in our reproductive rights. Of course, there are still discriminatory situations that occur each day. We've made progress but still not enough.

Radical feminists always existed in secret pockets of the movement. Over time, they infiltrated and became more vocal. As a result, feminism has changed to promote the ideology of female control as opposed to equal opportunity and the infectious spirit loves to attach to women wounded by men in their past. It lurks in chat rooms, work places, and homes just waiting for the opportunity to inhabit a female being to carry out its corrupt and divisive agenda.

In the late 19th century, women of color who were activists for women's rights differentiated themselves from white feminists and referred to themselves as womanists. While the movements were similar, women of color felt that their needs were different. Many of them tried to partner with their white counterparts to further the cause but found it to not be a productive venture. Just imagine their thoughts on the radical feminist movement.

The radical feminist movement has perpetuated the myth of the Superwoman to the extent that it tainted a woman's role in society. Modern day feminists say, "*I can do anything a man can do.*" Some even have a more extreme viewpoint, "*I can do anything a man can do and I can do it better.*" Personally, I'd like to know what we have to prove. From my vantage point, absolutely nothing! The "powers that be" benefit from unequal treatment of supposed minorities. While feminism is a noble quest, it's not worth the effort to deal with Neanderthal mentality. Certainly, men can't do everything women can do, so why should the reverse be true? To restore order, we must eradicate the Superwoman myth and embrace the principles of divine balance.

Independent Woman Syndrome

INDEPENDENT WOMAN Syndrome is a manmade phenomenon. It exists because we're living in a perpetual state of mistrust and we avoid interdependent relationships. Lack of trust is only one reason the epidemic is so prevalent. Another reason is the limited male population in comparison to the number of women in this country. Lastly, a systematic emasculation of men of color has taken over. This is due to incarceration, drug addiction, and the Superwoman state of mind that mentally hinders even the available men.

What is an independent woman? Is she simply a hard worker who has it all together or is she one who depends upon no one other than herself? Let's start by defining the term *independent*. According to the Merriam Webster dictionary, the definition of *independent* is as follows.

- Not dependent,

- Not subject to control by others,

- Self-governing, not affiliated with a larger control-ling unit,

- Not looking to others for one's opinions or for guidance in conduct,

- Not requiring or relying on others (as for care or livelihood,

- Showing a desire for freedom.

For a free-spirited woman like me, that definition is divine. At the same time, I'm mindful that radical feminists and women scorned have manipulated this freedom and turned it into man hate. It's one thing to handle your business. It's another thing to spread poison about our male counterparts because of bad experiences. Instead, we should be working to bind the spirit that attracts abusive men and loose divine companionship in our lives. Unfortunately, many of us are afraid to delve into the metaphysical aspects of relationships and wonder why we keep repeating the same sick cycle that keeps us imbalanced.

One of my good friends posted the following question as her status on a popular social networking site. "*What is your definition of an independent woman?*" The variety of responses sparked a juicy debate that went on for a few days. Some people felt it was acceptable for women to be independent. Others felt it went against divine principles. There were still others who were undecided yet felt they should include their indecision in the discussion. Even though this was a great dialogue, I was inclined to dig a little deeper. While on my journey for clarity, I coined the phrase *Independent Woman Syndrome* to describe the state of the female caught in the matrix. The matrix is all about distractions and that's why it's easy for women who have something to prove to get caught up in competing with men. I'm not suggesting that women should be so dependent upon their spouse, significant other, family, and friends to the extent that they lose sight of their own thoughts and feelings. Instead, I am advocating for being interdependent with humankind.

No woman is an island. God designed both women and men to depend upon one another. When we try to take the weight of life, all on our own, it can cause a serious imbalance. In the corporate world, the CEO is responsible for vision and strategy. The goal is to inspire and motivate corporate leaders to buy into and carry out that vision so the company can experience positive business results. Even though this is matrix mentality, it makes sense. If the associates have to do their job along with the job of the CEO, they would not be very productive. The associate's role is to be tactical. Being tactical and strategic at the same time causes associates to play two different roles. Why should associates play the CEO's role when the company pays the CEO to do the job? Relating that concept to imbalance, how do we become beings who are interdependent with humankind? Here are a few examples of interdependent relationships.

- A married couple depends upon one another to take care of their family and home.

- Mechanics fix our cars when they are in need of repair. We pay them for their services.

- Friends are there when we want to celebrate or when we need a shoulder to cry on. We do the same for them in return.

- Parents care for their children and teach them the ways of life. Children bring their parents joy and help them leave a legacy.

Every human has a gift or a talent that compliments the others. If you are acting independently, you're not aligned with the cosmos and your energy if off. You'll be taking on tasks and activities that are outside of the realm of your responsibility, which creates a low vibration in the spirit realm to affect your state of balance. This causes others not be accountable for their role in society, families, or work life. Believe it or not, this may result in arrested development in that particular area of life for the other person.

Rejecting independence ideology is the simplistic key to recognizing why you may be out of balance. This leg of your journey to find life balance will initially be challenging, yet it will pay off in the end. Your dividends equate to the peace you're seeking. Most likely, it is the reason you decided to read this book.

The American Dream

ALMOST EVERY U.S. citizen wants to achieve the American dream. To make this happen, we tend to work our fingers to the bone. As employers demand more time, prices get higher, and children get more involved in activities, our lives tend to spin out of balance. What is the American Dream? The original idea was that we all should be able to achieve according to our ability. As time went on, people polluted it to define how many children and cars we should have and how prosperous we should be. Our current society reflects the idea that there is no limit on this dream.

The ever chasing of the American dream robs us of precious family time, which is necessary to stay in one accord. Something as simple as eating dinner together at a family table can become an extreme challenge if both parents hold down jobs, one or both work overtime, and they are trying to figure out who is going to pick up little Johnny from soccer and Susie from track practice. We must stay in our lane to pursue our purpose.

When we do things that aren't in the flow of our purpose, we're out of alignment, which causes imbalance. Many of us have no choice but to work and we should never allow it to take so much of our time that we neglect our spiritual practices and family To live a balanced life, we must redefine the American dream according to spiritual standards.

Balance Check

• • •

Have you ever referred to yourself as a Superwoman? What was your reason?

What are your thoughts on the difference between a Superwoman and a balanced woman?

How do you identify with the women's rights movements, whether feminism, womanism, or radical feminism?

How have these movements been a benefit to you? How have they been harmful?

Do you consider yourself an independent woman?

If yes, how does that impact being interdependent with others?

How has trying to achieve the American Dream impacted your balance?

Moment of Reflection

• • •

What are three key points you'll take away from these sections on Superwoman is for Girls and The Origin of Imbalance?

A State of Balance

• • •

Prelude

IN SCIENCE class, we learned the all of the earth's energy comes from the sun. It's also imperative that the radiation that enters the atmosphere through sun rays is sent back to space. The earth's energy balance must be in check to make sure this process occurs. That's why we have high and low temperatures and seasons. Similarly, we must balance our energy by being mindful of what we absorb and radiate into the atmosphere.

To obtain true balance, it's important to know what "balance' means. For our purposes, let's focus on three snippets from the definition in the Merriam Webster's dictionary.

- Power to decide,

- State of emotional equilibrium,

- Harmonious arrangement,

In the next few chapters, we'll examine each one in detail and reveal the secrets to achieve a state of balance.

Power to Decide

A S WOMEN, we have the power to decide what we want to do with our lives. We can live one that's balanced or one that's imbalanced. It's our choice. This liberation is our God-given gift. Unfortunately, it doesn't always seem that way. Almost as if, someone or something else is always in control of our time. Most women still find it challenging to balance family time, spiritual practices, jobs, cleaning, cooking, and other activities. It seems like we need the force of an army to do all of the things that are on our plate.

How do balanced women make decisions about how to spend their time? Do they have some sort of special criteria or process? Yes indeed, they do and it's not complicated. A balanced woman understands the noble purpose for her family and weighs each decision to see how it aligns. What is a noble purpose? It's what you exist to do. In this case, what your family exists to do. I heard one family say their purpose is to shine a light on positive relationships in their community. Another family shared that they are together to show the world how blended families should operate.

Some of you know your noble purpose and haven't formally stated it or discussed it with your family. Either way, set aside some time to have that conversation with your family. Let them know that it's important to know this information and use it as a guide in decisions that you all make. If you're the only person in your family, it should be an easy process because you don't have to confer with anyone but yourself. No matter what size your family may be, have the discussion, write the noble purpose, and use it to make decisions. That's how you enact the power to decide.

Emotional Equilibrium

WITHOUT PROPER balance, your emotions can breed negative outcomes in your life. Fear, insecurity, confusion, offense, anger, hurt, rejection, being misunderstood, and a host of other counter-positive emotions aren't divine. To ensure that you're walking in balance, don't allow negative emotions to rule your mind. In other words, make time to take care of yourself.

The "powers that be" require a work force so that they can sit back and collect the cash. For this reason, they use marketing and rigid work structures to encourage us to fill our bodies with junk food and our minds with pointless activity. This keeps us away from home and far from learning the truth about ourselves. Then we fall into a state of guilt and shame about what we're not doing right. Because we can't see clearly, we become willing citizens in the matrix and live unproductive lives. I call this the *matrix mentality*. A mentality designed to promote legal slavery and prevent you from pursuing your divine purpose.

How we avoid falling into the matrix mentality? What steps should we take to adopt a new pattern of thinking? I suggest three actions; stimulate and rest your mind, nourish your body, and and feed your soul through intentional care. Let's explore each action.

Stimulate and Rest Your Mind

It's important to ensure that you have a balance of mental stimulation and rest. Otherwise, you'll find yourself an emotional wreck. *Mental stimulation* involves the following.

- Read books about health, wellness, and spirituality

- Solve logic puzzles

- Play logic games

- Have healthy debates

- Research your favorite subject

- Create a family tree

- Play your favorite instrument.

Mental rest is important because our minds need down time to recuperate from the high stress of the day. Here are a few examples to help you in the area of mental care.

- Meditate.

- Engage in breathing exercises.

- Listen to soft, relaxing music.

- Sit by a refreshing stream of water or the fireplace.

- Practice yoga or Tai Chi.

- Talk with a spiritual counselor.

- Explore options like the Emotional Freedom Technique.

- Find what works for you stick to it and grow.

Mental stimulation and rest builds your brainpower and clears your mind. Focusing here gives you the ability to distinguish between God's voice and that of people.

Nourish Your Body

Physical activity is imperative to our survival. It ensures proper functioning of the body and mind. Without it, toxins and acids lay dormant in our body, releasing improper hormones that cause us to be tired, cranky, emotional, and not as productive as we could be. For this reason, it's a good idea to incorporate some sort of aerobic activity into your life daily. We should engage in this type of activity at least 30 minutes, three to four times per week. Here are a few suggestions to get you moving and back on track.

- Take a walk after lunch and/or dinner.

- Have dance time or play physical games with the family after dinner.

- Walk around the track or field while your children are at football, soccer, or cheerleading practice.

- Stretch and/or jog in place while watching your favorite TV show.

- Ride the recumbent bike or walk on the treadmill while watching your favorite television show.

- Go on a hike with your family and/or friends.

- Work in your personal or community garden.

Feed Your Spirit

Emotionally balanced women take the time to establish a relationship with God beyond church, meeting, or temple attendance. The focus is building a relationship with the creator of the universe. This can consists of the following actions.

- Pray

- Meditate

- Sing songs from your heart

- Dance

- Read and/or study spiritual books

- Simply soak in God's presence

The last recommendation is one of my favorites. We're typically so busy that we miss the simple things in life. In fact, when I share this concept with women, many of them don't feel comfortable doing nothing at all. One of my relatives told me, "You should never just sit around and do nothing. There's always something that needs to be done around the house. If not, you should be helping someone else." I lived according to that mentality for many years and eventually suffered from being chronically tired. On top of my busy lifestyle, I didn't eat right and enjoyed baking sweet goodies for myself and others. Cheesecakes, brownies, pound cakes, German chocolate cakes, and chocolate chip cookies were my claim to fame. I managed a team at a Fortune 100 corporation and had my teenage son in a million activities, too.

Once I figured out I needed to rest, I started doing things like watching birds, gazing at the moon on a clear night, having a cup of herbal tea on the patio, or just sitting in a park and observing God's creation. In the summer months, I'd do a few of these things on my lunch break. These are just a few ways to simply soak in God's presence. No matter where you choose to do it, just be still. Make sure you're "being" and not "doing" so that you can hear the whisper of God.

Harmonious Arrangement

J UST IMAGINE if you went to the symphony and their in-
struments were out of tune. Even worse, what if they played
off beat? When we complain, gossip, yell, and compete, we
change the energy in our space from positive to negative. From
a metaphysical perspective, you attract the same type of energy
you give off. If you continually emit negative energy, you'll attract it. Eventually, the weight of the negative energy will send
your body into overload, resulting in sickness and depression.

To play in a symphony, musicians are required to practice
so that the harmonies and melodies blend perfectly. If you
played an instrument and had trouble hitting a certain note,
you'd either practice or get a coach to help you achieve your
goal. The same applies to maintaining positive energy. It's
important that we practice being positive in the same manner.
That may require getting outside assistance from a life coach.

Imagine that your body is a bank account. Positive energy equals a deposit, while negative energy equates to a withdrawal. No one is perfect and we all have negative moments. The goal is to balance our or have an overflow. We can live an average life and just have a zero balance or we can have an overflow and live life to the fullest.

Balance Check

• • •

What is your family's purpose?

How do you and your family communicate about this purpose?

How are the activities you're involved aligned with this purpose?

If you're not involved in any activities, should you be involved in one that fulfills your family's purpose? If so, what is it?

Moment of Reflection

• • •

What are three key points you'll take away from this section on State of Balance?

Balance Enhancements

• • •

Prelude

W'VE EXPLORED how our lives get out of balanced, defined the word, learned some new ways to live a balanced life. When we graduate from high school, we either go on to college or enter the workforce full time. Just because we left school doesn't mean that we stopped learning. Similarly, getting to a place of balance requires us to continually learn more about it. That's why it's important to learn a few ways to enhance your balanced state.

Like graduate and professional courses, the learning has taken place and now it's time for some practice and implementation.

Spiritual Alignment

WHEN A car is out of balance, there's a negative impact on its performance and an alignment is necessary to correct it. Once the mechanic realigns the wheels, the car is in balance, significantly reducing wear and tear. It's a good idea to get periodic alignments, as well. The beauty of all is that your car will ride smoother and the amount of gas burned decreases, which puts cash back into the owner's pocket.

Similarly, a spiritual alignment reduces wear and tear on our emotional equilibrium to promote healing of deep wounds that cause us to be imbalanced. We can seek God for an emotional healing but that's only one part of the process. In order to function in wholeness, we need to take action to heal our emotional wounds and fortify them against potential ruptures. We do this by saying *positive affirmations*, replacing our old negative thoughts with new divine ones.

What are positive affirmations? They are statements that affirm the positive aspects of who you are and what you'll accomplish. God created the world to operate in a such a way that when we speak things into the atmosphere, the universe responds on our behalf. As a result, God touches hearts and minds to open doors for that were previously closed. This type of thinking is foreign to some and blasphemy for others. It takes a spiritually mature person to understand how God commands the universe and give us power to do the same in regards to our purpose and destiny.

I remember watching the cartoon He-Man as a child. When the main character would turn into He-Man, he held up a sword and said the words, "By the powers of the universe . . ." I remember thinking, "There ain't (yes I said ain't) no power in the universe. He better call on God." Years later it dawned on me that God created the universe by speaking it into existence. We're made in God's image, which speaks to the spirit in each of us. That spirit has divine power and when we access it, nothing is impossible.

This brings to mind a song I used to sing with my son during his younger years, by The Clark Sisters. One line of the song says, "The sky is the limit to what I can have. Just believe and receive it and God will perform it today." I sing this song when I get discouraged and can't see the God giving me the power to speak over my life. It reminds me that I have access of tools and resources to soar like an eagle. I just have to be open to going beyond the traditional walls of religion to receive them.

One of the reasons I live a balanced life is that I get to write books and do consulting work, two of my passions. If I hated my job, I'm not sure that balance would come to me so easily. So how do you get there if you're not in my situation? Speaking positive affirmations is an imperative practice to obtain balance balance. These words will help the spiritual powers align on your behalf. I remember my first day of working at a major corporation after graduating from college. I'd spoke about my goals so much that people knew I wanted to write books and work as a consultant. Of course, it didn't happen overnight, yet I gained the necessary experience and made the right connections as I followed the whisper of God. Doors opened for me that I never could have fathomed all on my own.

Even cars with realigned wheels require ongoing maintenance. Once we've mastered the art of speaking positive affirmations, it's important to avoid falling into a stagnant state. Its human nature to believe that mastery doesn't require continued growth. We do it all of the time. For example, we learn about spiritual practices or the business we're supposed to start, see some good results, become complacent, and stop. The key is to stop being satisfied with average growth and seek exponential growth.

The matrix society frowns upon this because people who grow exponentially refuse to allow anyone or anything to control and manipulate them. Know this. As you grow, folks will challenge you. Even though they respect what you're doing, they may not understand it or they may be upset. The reality is that they don't believe in the concept of exponential growth beyond their own mental walls and barriers brought on by systematic societal control mechanisms.

Another way to align spiritually and achieve optimal balance is to eat electric foods that cleanse the body to promote an environment for optimal wellness. When I decided to live a holistic lifestyle, I either eliminated or extremely reduced the use of products with preservatives, synthetic ingredients, and refined sugars and flours. In addition, I significantly decreased my meat intake and shared goals of eventually living a vegan life. A few family members and friends supported my efforts and even asked how they could change their lives. Others thought I'd gone stone cold crazy and snickered about my efforts. Over the years, I get stronger in the ability to stand on my own due to the experiences I've encountered.

At one family gathering, someone offered a donut to me and I turned it down. The funny thing was that I turned it down due to donuts giving me heartburn, which I discovered prior to my conversion. So my decline had nothing to do with my new lifestyle. I heard someone (who's name I won't mention) snicker and say, "I bet she'd eat it if you told her it was organic." I just smiled and kept it moving. I refuse to be around folks caught up in the matrix to the extent that they have to down others.

At the next station, one of my cousins asked, "Does that mean you're going to stop making those brownies?"

I responded with, "I can make brownies, still. The ingredients might be a little different though."

She chuckled and whispered to another cousin, "I don't want those kind of brownies. I want some real brownies like she used to make."

I laughed to myself because I couldn't believe that she considered organic and natural ingredients to not be "real." Instead, the matrix sold her a bill of goods that synthetic and refined ingredients were real. If people took charge of their own health, then the food industry would bottom out and people would know what it means to eat "real" food instead of massive amounts of refined sugar and flour, soy, animal protein, and wheat. These ingredients tear our bodies to shreds and rip us of precious energy while adding the taste we're programmed to crave and shelf life that makes the big bucks for corporations who produce these goods.

While my journey isn't a perfect one, I'm growing more and more each day. I had to put aside the thoughts and opinions of others and do what was right for me. This led me to a path that God designed specifically for me. Following the right path leads to the following benefits.

- You will obtain mental clarity.

- You will know which tasks to take on.

- You will know which tasks to delegate.

- You will know which tasks not to do.

- You will set clear and reasonable boundaries.

- Your work will yield fruit.

- You will have better health.

- Your stress level will decrease.

All of these benefits promote a balanced lifestyle. So align your spirit with positive energy to have exponential growth and phenomenal results.

Mental Colonic

THE THEME of balance enhancements is centered around the words we speak. In fact, much of our imbalance has nothing to do with overloaded schedules and tasks. There can be issues brought on by the words, ancient promises, and bloodlines curses. That's why we need a mental colonic to cleanse us of every **word curse**, **casual covenant**, or **negative agreement**. Let's take a moment to establish definitions of the phrases.

A **word curse** takes place when someone spouts out negative words about you that get in the way of your destiny. Some examples of a word curse are, *"You're just like your father." "You'll never be anything in life." "You'll never be as good as your brother/sister."* Word curses cancel out our God-given blessings unless they are reversed in deed and action.

A **casual covenant** is a verbal agreement with negative

energy about your current and/or future state of mind. An example of a casual covenant is "*I'm sick and tired*." Once you put this statement into the atmosphere, you find yourself literally being sick and tired. Another example is saying, "*I'm never going to get married*." In many cases, people speak their spinsterhood into existence simply through the words they say. These words can frame their mindset, which will affect how they approach the various aspects of life. Eventually, the words will manifest in the natural realm.

A **negative agreement** is your personal agreement with a word curse. Here's an example. Imagine that your family has a history of an illness like high blood pressure. You take medication, live with a defeated perspective, and continually tell yourself you'll always have to take medicine for high blood pressure because it runs in your family.

In our matrix mentality, we're open to negative spirits that speak word curses, casual covenants, and negative agreements to us in first person. When we hear the words in this manner, we tend to mistake the thoughts for our own.

As I was writing the business plan for *Refreshing Streams, Inc.*, I was nervous because it was a new endeavor. During this time, the enemy put thoughts in my head in first person. For example, "*I can't do this because I don't have enough connections*." Another thought that plagued me for several days was even worse, "*I am never going to get my book finished, so how in the world can I open a publishing company*." These types of thoughts continued to pop into my mind until I actually spoke them aloud. Why did I speak them aloud? I actually started to believe these discouraging thoughts. I actually stopped writing and planning for several weeks because the thoughts were so debilitating.

One day, God showed me that these thoughts weren't mine. They were part of the negative energy from the matrix. I began to cancel each of these thoughts and bind the power they had over my mind. I declared that I would finish this book and that *Refreshing Streams, Inc.* would be a success.

I declared that I would have the necessary focus to make it happen. I decreed that the spiritual atmosphere would line up to be in my favor and that the negative hosts tormenting my mind be bound and sent to the pit where they belonged.

Once I removed all of the matrix clutter, I refilled my mind with a new substance; positive affirmations. I wrote down all of the things I believed about my success and began to speak them daily until they were deep in my heart. I also implemented the principle of binding and loosing. I called the statements that came out of my mouth **Chain Breaking Affirmations** and I even wrote a few of them down. Here's an example.

Through the power of God in me, I bind the spirit of
_____ (i.e. poverty, addiction, infir-
mity, cancer, etc.). I cut off its connection to my family and
me in the second Heaven. I call the angelic hosts to drag the
matrix energy out in chains. Confine it to the abyss from
which it came and forbid it's reentrance into my life. I loose
_____ (i.e. generational blessings,
prosperity, unconditional love, purity, etc.) over my family and
myself. Through the power of God, I declare and decree that
we will be free from matrix bondage. I declare and decree that
my emotions will be stabilized and that stress and life issues
will no longer bog me down.

One ploy of the matrix society is to make you believe that you have no power and authority to stop the spiritual attacks on your life. This teaching has even morphed over time to the thought that if you believe in certain deities, the negative spiritual forces can't harm you. Yet another teaching touts the idea that the spirit realm doesn't exist. It's just a figment of our imagination. These teachings are quite far from the truth. While connecting with God gives you an advantage over and insight into the spirit realm, we must take intentional action to clear the atmosphere around us. Spiritual realignments must take place daily so that we continue to grow in power and strength.

Guilt Detox

THE DELIBERATING spirit of guilt digs its roots and tentacles into our souls, trying to cling to almost every thought, action, and decision. Its goal is to keep us in spiritual bondage to prevent us from living an abundant life. Guilt is comprised of "feelings of culpability especially for imagined offenses or from a sense of inadequacy."

It tends to enter your life through the following ways.

- **Manipulation:** Guilt oftentimes gets a foothold in our lives when a manipulative person wants us to do something for them and, if we're not able to do it, that person may respond by saying, "You don't love me." "You'll need me before I need you." Or, "You always put everything else before me."

- **Immoral Acts**: When a person commits an immoral act such as taking drugs, lying, or harming others, they open the door to the spirit of guilt. Especially if the immoral act is addictive in nature. I've heard drug addicts share the guilt they feel every time they smoke or shoot up.

- **Approval seeking**: People want to hear, "well done" when they accomplish certain goals or perform certain acts. They make look from that validation from significant others, spouses, parents, friends, teachers, or bosses. The basic desire to be recognized for our accomplishments is healthy. It becomes toxic when we do what others say just to get their approval. This perverted desire keeps us from truly walking in our purpose and can lead to the spirit of guilt when the desired approval isn't obtained.

When we eliminate the guilt factor, we prevent getting caught up in a cycle of emotional bondage. In the following scenario, a mother and business woman struggles to handle conflicting priorities and emotional guilt trips. Try to put yourself in her shoes to determine how you would handle the situation.

Sarah is a marketing executive and the mother of two young boys. She is engaged to their father, Ted, and they're planning a wedding. On this particular day, Sarah needed to take the boys to guitar lessons after work then meet with Ted and the wedding planner.

Moments before the scheduled meeting, Sarah's boss, Kendra, dropped into her office unexpectedly. She frantically shared that she needed help with a presentation for the corporate board. The deck was due to the Communications Consultant in the morning. Since Sarah's staff members were gone for the day, Kendra had the nerve to ask Sarah to stay late and work on the slide deck.

Feeling overwhelmed, Sarah took a deep breath. This wasn't about conflicting priorities. This was about bad planning on Kendra's part. She decided to be transparent and share her schedule conflict. To Sarah's dismay, Kendra snapped at her, insisted she put her job first, and reminded her of all the times she allowed her to leave early for other family obligations. Sarah fumed in her mind and managed to maintain her composure.

Feeling like she had no other option, Sarah caved under the pressure and called her fiancé to explain the situation. Maybe he could take the boys to their guitar lesson, even though he took them to soccer practice for the past few evenings. They could always reschedule the meeting with the planner, right? Of course, Ted didn't respond in a positive manner and was angry at Sarah's decision. He felt she was putting her job before their children and their wedding plans. She felt guilty because now both her boss and fiancé pulled her in different directions.

What would you do in Sarah's situation? Would you tell Kendra to go fly a kite and stick to your plans or would you just give in? There's a happy medium here. Sarah could use the template from a previous board presentation to cut design time in half and take her laptop to the children's guitar lesson since the teacher insists that parents aren't in the room during the sessions. By doing this, she'll still be able to get the deck started for her boss who can finish the rest.

Sarah proposed this idea to Kendra and she readily accepted. She grabbed a few reports she'd need to use as content for the presentation, saved the template to her hard drive, and left to pick up the boys.

This is just one example of how someone can try to flip a guilt trip on you. Most people end up feeling so badly that they just do what the person wants. When they don't, they leave the interaction feeling bad, allowing unnecessary emotions to cloud their vision. Guilt and balance cannot live in the same body. One must give in to the other and I advocate for balance every time.

Balance Check

• • •

Moment of Reflection

● ● ●

What are three key points you'll take away from these sections on Balance Enhancements?